SONGS OF A FAR-WALKING WOMAN...

by

Maggie Smith

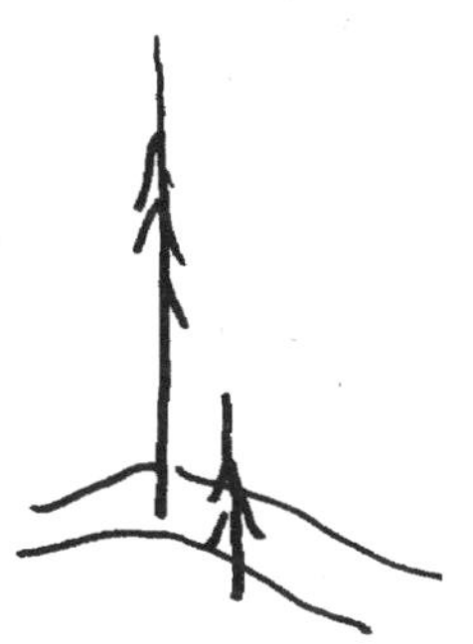

NEW ENERGY PRESS
MINNEAPOLIS
1996

Contents

Part One

Part Two

Her poetry is a view from inside the tumult. She gives us glimpses of the people struggling with forces well beyond their understanding and helps us sense those forces as well. Her voice is lyrical in that it is the deeply personal expression of her intuition and her understanding of a world which is always in the present but carries the full burden of its history.

This collection is organized to follow an ever-widening discovery of the world. Part One includes the poems which focus on the discovery of nature. Part Two is devoted to the city and the world of business. Part Three catches people in a moment of their history. Part Four moves to the search for answers to questions that thread through all our lives.

Maggie Smith's poetry is not about her life. It is her life. It is the way she has of understanding, not only the world she sees, but the world she knows, intuitively, is there. It is a way of seeing and feeling which can help us all.

Foreword

Maggie Smith is an American original. She has been shaped and molded by the events of her generation, but her voice is her own. The poetry reflects threads in a life which began on the prairies of southern Alberta, Canada where the wide skies meet, in the far distance, the undulating brown hills, unfenced and untracked. Her life began when pioneer life was only a generation away. The simple values of the wilderness were still available and the lessons of the harshness of nature were all around her. A heritage of a Cree grandmother, a Scottish grandfather, and forebearers who fought in the American Revolution connected her to the history of her land.

But the poems also reflect the movement away from that simple pioneer struggle to the complicated world of business, technology, and the human struggle for values which are lost and found in a complex world. Maggie Smith is a part of that world, sometimes wistful for the simplicity of the wilderness, but participating in and understanding the new changes that flow from technological miracles and social engineering. She seeks to find the spiritual truths in a world that muffles the rhythms of spirituality.

A Dedication

To all those who have accompanied me
along the way, my thanks for your
love and support.

To Margaret, my daughter, always a joy,
and Eva and Adrian
who are just beginning to sing
their own songs.

Poetry and Drawings

by

Maggie Smith

Cover Design
by
Gary Hansen

Cover Photography
by
Bob Olsgard

The suggestions of Craig and Kathy Little
and Norma Cudd in reviewing the manuscript
are gratefully acknowledged.

Publisher's Cataloging in Publication
(Prepared by Quality Books Inc.)

Smith, Maggie E.
Songs of a far-walking woman / by Maggie Smith
p. cm.
ISBN 0-9642979-1-4

I. Title.
PS3569.M344266 1996 811'.54
QB195-20661

Part Three

Part Four

A Note From Maggie

My life began on a Canadian prairie as flat and empty as Japanese paper before the brush. But its very emptiness allowed me to see the tiny growing things and the far distant flight of birds. We had a sheepherder on our ranch who would recite long poems for me. Some of them were of his own making; some were from the Scottish poets of the nineteenth century. My mother and father read to me from an early age, and words took on a sense long before I saw their shapes or spelling. Once I had learned to read, I read voraciously and the works of the major poets of the world held a deep attraction for me. I found myself at home with their ways and in awe of their skill and insight.

For me, writing poetry has always been an important means of communication. The poetry I write is a dialogue with myself, with a friend, with an author, or with God. Poetry is more than the words. The stops and pauses, the runs and colors of poetry allow for a story to be shared, a memory explored or a hope to be expressed that is not limited by the mere words of prose.

Poetry is also a discovery for me. When I am moved by a scene, an event or a person, I explore that emotion in poetry. The poems in this collection are those discoveries which have accumulated over several decades.

As I look back on the decades of my life, I get a sense of the distances I have traveled but there has never been a straight path to a goal. My husband once said of me, "Margaret never gets lost. She just changes her destination." There is more truth to that than I often like to admit. In searching for a title for this collection, I wanted something which would convey that sense of movement in life. I found it in a discussion with an Ojibwa man that I chanced to meet. We were comparing where we had come from and where our paths might have crossed. After a short review of the places I had lived, he shook his head and said,

"You're a far-walking woman!"

And so I am. And these are the songs I sang along the way.

Maggie Smith
Minneapolis, MN

1

AFTER THE STORM

The sunlight in the frosty air
Reflecting on the branches bare
Is all too bright to be so still.

Yesterday across the snow,
I saw a silver whirlwind blow
A blue-cupped chalice in the hill.

A drinking cup for such as he
Who came from out the Arctic ice
And played wild songs upon a harp
Brought from the land of Thrace.

How quiet and how bright this day.
Last night...
I would have followed him away.

ATHABASCA

The Great Slave lies
In the arms of the Swan
And hills are still in a dream.
On the edge of the world
Where I was born...
The Bow was a widening stream.

My mother Cree
Wells up in me...
I smell the muskeg burning.
The same wind blows
From the northern snows
And brings the geese returning...

But for me
It cannot be.

No southern spring
Can ever bring
Such wonder.
Nor can slow unfold
The tamarack's pale green and gold
That mingles with the smokes
Which rise against the sky,
Entangled with the geese that fly...

A web to catch me
With its hope...

Be still my heart!
Do not start
At the wind
From the northern slope...

Already have the oil and gold
Begun their siren song...
I love you deeply, wilderness
But you will not linger long...

And I am caught.

The baited trap
Of the city street
With its food and comfort,
Sure and neat,
Will hold me
Though the evening sky
Re-echoes...

Like a coyote's cry.

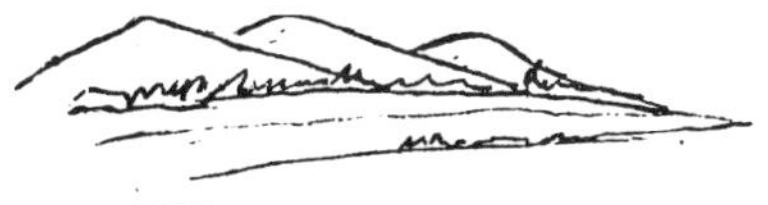

WINTER MOON

The game is scarce
The field is ice.
The owl swoops low
In search of mice.
The rabbits track
Is rare indeed.
The timberwolf
Cries loud his need
The branches crackle
With the frost...

The cold can kill
The man who's lost!

FEBRUARY

February, Bill
Is the second month
Time when the Year
Discovers she is pregnant...

It does not show
Beneath the ice corset.
Her figure is contained
All its pure and smooth
        White snow.

Folded and draped it is.

But there are strange stirrings
Of tulip bulbs
And secretive
Small nippled buds
Enlarging
To the song
Of street sparrows...

        Bill,
        February is a woman's month.
        Love her for that.

AS LONG AS THE EARTH LASTS

As long as the earth lasts, I shall be
A young and laughing thing...

For every Winter that I die,
I live another Spring.

When Winter takes my life away,
I smile most secretly.
And then I rise, and change my coat
And let my hair flow free...

For every Winter that I pay,
The earth gives Spring to me.

THE DEEDED SCROLL

This land I claim.
        That sky is mine.
And all the laughter
        Of the birds
That swoop above the bridge.
        And all the grass

        This scroll is hidden
Till the legislators of the mind
        And all their books shall pass
        Into oblivion.

And then shall I
        Unthread the ribbons
        Of my sky
And walk, new owner of the blue
From hill to hill
        In step with you.

DROUGHT

There was no snow this year
        And all the earth lay open.
A child abandoned in the street
        Without a coat and naked feet,
The earth was.
                And the air was dry with fear,
While dust and smoke rose up
        And rode upon the wind
        Day after day...

Spring came softly once
        And went away.

And then I saw a single bird
        Fly up toward the only cloud gone by
To seed it with his song of silver...
        By this cry,
                This ancient deed of alchemy,
The rain began!

The arid earth
Did rise and suck
The turgid nipples of the rain,
And children ran
To wade in water
As before...
Laughing
They were.

And from the door, upon the lawn,
I saw pink-lipped apple blossoms.

Winter's gone!

BORA BORA

Most beautiful place,
If place it is,
Or did I swim in a dream?

The water is warm as my blood
And green as my emerald is green.

The sky is silver refined.
The air is still as my mind.

But if I turn my head, I hear
The roar of ocean
Against the farthest reef.
It's sounds become the cries of grief
That I have left behind.
No...
  I cannot hide in heaven.
    I am of humankind.

A LOOK AT THE STARS NEAR AYERS ROCK, AUSTRALIA

Through tall grass and sand,
We walked to banks of telescopes
That scanned the southern heavens.
I knew the Southern Cross would be
A different guide...
I knew familiar stars would change
Their face or hide.

We watched the sudden tropic night
As all around the stars exploded into light!

Then all at once, a chaos
New to me, a focus far
From all my common world:

> Rolling planets! Bursting stars!
> Great furnaces of power
> That even in their dying hour
> Continue to devour
> The space between infinities.

I stared transfixed at these

Dark change and terror ride
Round the galaxies of suns,
Wing to wing.

And these are interlocked upon the air
In great concentric circles
Where the sine
Is analogued to infinite design
Of hirographic, high, hypnotic rings
That hold me motionless.

I cannot move or talk.
I am like the rabbit
Shadowed by the hawk.

I have forgot
The little beaded, separate days
That string my life.
I only see this awful brilliance
That can blind the soul
And linger like the aftercall
Of some great bird of prey
That seeks a riper carrion
But was warned away.

This early light of far Eternity
Has changed me.

As, looking past the darkened bars,
I long for Dante's God of Love
That moves the sun
And all the other stars.
The still small voice of He
Who also turns the wheel of human things.

I need the smile of friends,
Black coffee and my coat to wear.

How strangely cold this desert air!

2

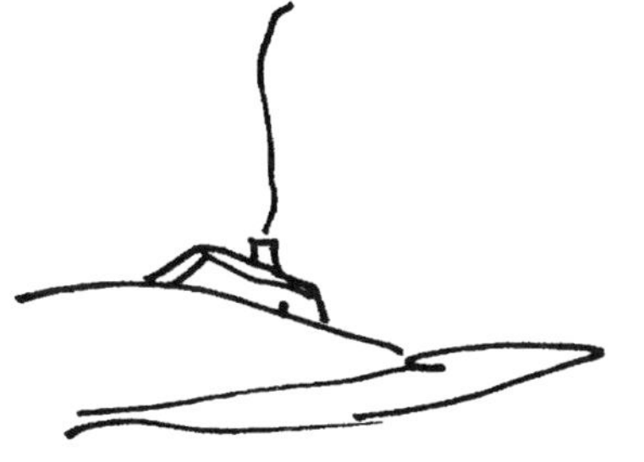

LORING PARK

Pale park in April
Where the sun
Pairs old men who play
Eternal checkers, and the day
Moves through squares
Of shade and light
Pursuing swallows
While a flight
Of April clouds
Wakes green buds of willows
There...
Where small boys cut bare
Slim wands for whistles
As they stare
At the antique woman
With the braided hair
Whose weak twig fingers
Reach for loam
From far off farmlands
That were once her home.

Uprooted still, she sits
Near this small field
And dreams
And reads,
Devoutly,
From a holy catalogue
Of seeds

THE WINDS OF WINTER

What will the winds of winter bring
Beyond bronze autumn's harvesting?
I draw the radar round me thrice
And wait the spirit's answering.

But no matter what I know
From science and the strange device,
The inborn fear of Arctic ice
That took from man his paradise
        A million years ago
        Still calls to me.

The earth, eternal, waits the blow
The fall of alabaster snow
        The cold.
        The blood
Of all the living seems to flow
        Reluctant
        Slow.
Even in the cities, forest law
Holds dominion till the thaw...

And the fine frivolity of Christmas tries
To hide this terror in men's eyes.
        This ancient knowledge that the earth
        Will not yield honey, nor give birth
        Until the sun is warm again...

Man will wait in his electric lair
Drawing pictures from the air
        Of April rain, and love songs
        Manufactured
        In New York...

All unconscious that he knows
A danger stirring his repose.
        Soft the question rides the air
        While the sun is warm and fair
        Like the perfume of a pear.

What will the winds of winter bring
Beyond bronze Autumn's harvesting?

        A stillness from the birds that go
        And foxes' fear of famine in the spring.

CHICAGO

I saw the city yesterday
Great long boulevards of grey,
With flashing lights
And costumes gay...
And windows full of wonder.
I saw the great high Tribune Tower,
        Above the sky train's
        Screaming power
        And wheels and rails of thunder.

And then I saw the stores close tight
And in the city's paler light
The bread and wine were hid from sight
Behind the crossbar's iron might
Excluding lust and hunger.

Dark was made for stars and moon
And scented grass and calling loon
And all the wonders hid from noon...

In that city strange, I saw
Fear walk naked of the law.
All the city's terror toys
Were clanging with a narrow
Noise
That drifted
Past the lake:
The roar of planes
The pour of cars...

Dark was made for stars.

THE TOURIST IN MEXICO

The Spanish church
Held riches greater than the town
It towered above the streets, and down
Its ornate ceilings there was gold.
The history and art were old.

But older still
The ancient Mayan shrine
Hidden deep
Below the altar pillars,
And its gods asleep.

In Britain too,
Some Christian altars stand
Above a pagan sacred place.
No longer rulers of the land
Are Mithras or the Celtic face.

I heard a soft, familiar sound.
A woman veiled was praying there.
And gentle was her evening prayer.
A gift of grace.
A quiet mind.
Old gods were
Left behind.

My sister at the altar
Warmly lit
By candleshine,
Your hopes are yours.
Your God is mine.

A TOURIST IN AUSTRALIA

Blue Mountains
And Blue Ocean.
        Sydney is a city of sunlight.

Her parks were planted
By the English
Two hundred years ago.
The tropic and the English trees
Have prospered
And they please
A world that comes
To buy and sell and marvel
At the distance

The British prison ships are history
And those who came
Are now First Families
And each name
Is proudly carried.

Old enemies -
The Germans and the Japanese
Have mingled with the Abo.
The opera house with sails of music
And the yachts that race
The hundred miles of coast
Are loved and followed
By the crowd.

The people surge and smile.
The sun warms all -
The harbor and the park.

But far below,
Dark water hides
The great White Shark.

STANDING STONES
IN ABERFELDIE, SCOTLAND

A ring of stones,
Three rows deep
In an old cow pasture
Below the big house...

A ring of stones,
Three thousand years the sun has set
And darkness cooled
And dew has wet.

Midsummer's day
Has warmed these stones,
And yet...
We know no more
Than mystery,
A little awe, a little fear...

We may return again
Next year.

AMERICA
1954

I do not know the battle
I do not feel the fear
But I have found the leaves are red
Much earlier this year.
Now I am not hungry
I have not grown old
But it is only August
And the wind is cold.

TEST BAN

The artist fingers of the man
Calculated atoms
And began
With his great mind to turn
        New worlds of wisdom
        Into numbers.
        Factorings of purple flame
        That bright began to burn
        In bursts of islands
        And to learn
        The depths of the Pacific sea.
Confirmed by the eclipses of the sun
And that strange death of fishermen
        In far Japan.

Not near to us...
Though rumors ran
Of radiation sickness.

How could we
Who ride the bus each morning
Or plant our golden corn
        Deep in the land of Lincoln
        Come to any harm?

Ah, but the air is free
And may carry death so lightly
From the testing grounds to me...

Death's prophets walk before her
With Geiger counter rod
Proclaiming she is coming
In all the names of God.

Dare we drink where trout lie cool
On pebbled bed in this land
Our fathers loved and can we eat the bread?
What will that great power defend
But nations of the blind and dead?

CENTERPIECE

The polished walnut table stands
        In cool magnificence.
Its silver bowl bears pears,
Bright yellow apples, plums, and peaches
But the bloom forswears
        All tenderness and truth.

Pale globes of false delight
I have Adam's appetite,
And the Serpent's singing lute
Wakes Eve's desire
For artificial fruit.

What promises it holds...
What wonders of the flesh...
Its very shape enfolds
The need for love and apples
And coats against the cold
Certainties of death.

Image graven in the dust
Shaped and crafted
Creature of our hand
You have become our world.

Do we understand?
We willed for love and apples
And they grew, a painted wax
Before our eyes.

Nor can we tell the true
From lies.

THOUGHTS ON THE NATURE OF MARBLE

This stone did Greece demand
And Rome carve out her heroes
Her marble votive stand
Before the Gods to pray...

This streamered surface stone
Is marked for praise alone...

But now is used for floors
And American toilet doors...

So much I cannot tell
If marble slabs
Have risen in the world
Or fell.

MIDAS

My eyes look up
And do not see,
        My heart beats loud
        And does not feel.
I've locked my life
And lost the key.
        Now I bow
        To money's heel.

CORPORATION SPIRIT

This eight-souled office
With a single mind
        This body meshed for profit
From the world
Is moving in its actions
Neither cruel nor kind.

Adding tapes and carbons
        In paper baskets curled
Are springs for motion.
Not hunger, sex, nor sleep,
But the deep, repeated clearing
Of Machines.

A corporation is a legal fiction
And the means
To rise more powerful than the
Single human, and it leans
On abstract owners' hopes
Of profit from the world.

A world whose lost communities
Are now restructured,
And their children cry
Alone in little rooms,
Far from the earth and sky.

This strange corporate spirit
Seeks a frame
Like those lost demons did of old
Who, driven out of their eternal sky
And hid in men and swine,
Finds they can neither live nor die
Except in fiction and in fame.

IT ISN'T THE GOLD...

Count the wealth
Of a thousand men.
Watch what men desire.
Know their thirst
And fear and pain.
See the rich
Go poor again.
Hear the bought
And the buyer
Cry with lust
And puff with power,
Sleek with feasting;
Their final hour
Distorted and twisted.
Greed and Pride
Cover a secret
They cannot hide:

It isn't the gold
And it isn't the gain.
It's ancient:
Wanting to walk in the rain,
Warm the hands by the fire,
Share bread and wine
With another soul
Before the funeral pyre.

But they walk blindly,
Lost in the maze
Of selfish lives
And separate days.

EPIPHANY

I have become
Too much aware
Of how the hound
Pursues the hare.

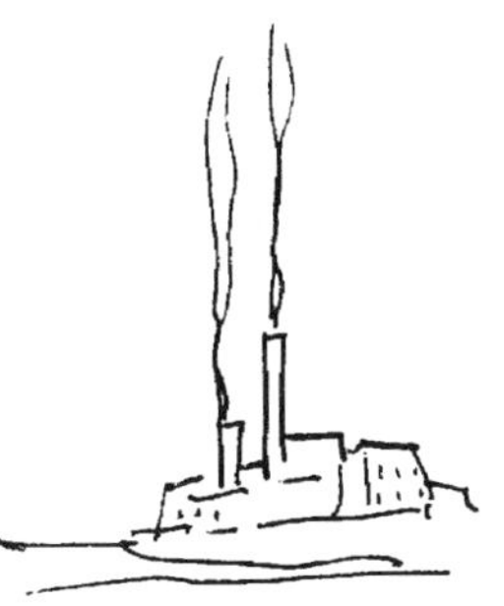

3

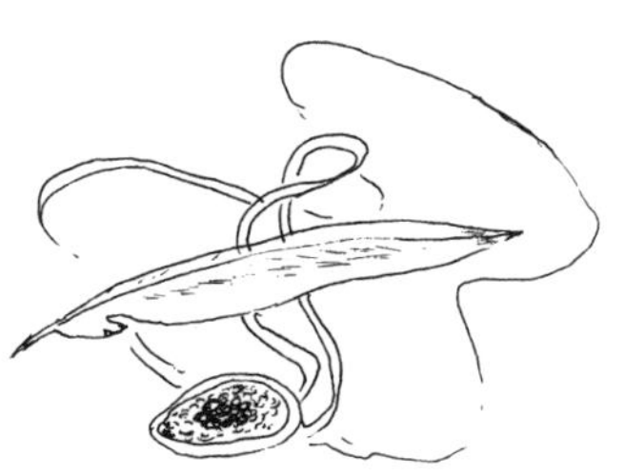

TUTSI WOMAN IN RHUWANDA 1994

"My husband and my sons are dead.
My father too. The land defiled,
But that is not the end of dread
I soon must bear a Hutu child."

Ages old, the fruit of war.
We in England
Knew the call,
A thousand years before.
"Vikings on the Eastern Shore."

My yellow hair
May tell you more.

ECHOES OF THE WAR

I burned the beef
We planned for supper.
So David said, "*Let's go out to eat,*
The smoke is bad.
It's hot this summer...
The odor's awful in this heat."

When we'd returned,
(We'd gone to dinner and a show)
"*That plane from Canada,*" he said.
His voice was conversational but low.
"*The bodies on the stretchers...*"
(For it had crashed and burned)
"*I saw the twisted arms and legs*
In the room when I returned."

A war that went away
Borne by the dead.

My husband remembers
The charred and outstretched
Arms of dead.
"*The odor was the same.*"
He said.

And then he read awhile
And went to bed.

GRANDMOTHER

Out of the night
You rise and stand,
A shadow figure
From shadow land.
Tall and straight
And calm and free
A sturdy heart within,
A Cree...

Your soul that never
Was shut in a cage
Is handing to me
A heritage...
No gift of gold
Or troublesome lands
But the easy burden
Of skillful hands.

RED LAKE MEN

I saw three men die.
Not those of the Cross,
The famous Three, our Christ and two thieves,
Back twenty centuries;
But men, obscure in their time, as These
Were obscure.

Men, this year
In shirts and jeans, Ojibwa men,
Not men of means.
Not in battle
But at home
Among the forest leaves.

All death is not heroic...
But these met on a battlefield of self
Won with courage,
Death with honor.
They were true
In their lives
To what they knew.

Harry was the first...
Grey and thin,
A woodsman, dead of cancer of the earth.
The spider web of pain, hour by hour,
Devoured him till his soul alone remained.

His son had carried him on his last hunt,
But "*The sights were off on the rifle.*"
The ancient hunting ground was his
And his the hiding place of deer.

The hunt brought out the question.
"*Across the road,*" he asked his wife
One day... "*Help me across the road.*
I do not want to go alone."

No one does.

A week before he died,
I came to him. He woke
And smiled in that strange bed,
And sang... as though he were a pipe
Of some forgotten pagan wood
The wind blew through.

He sang a love song...
He, one line, and I the next.
I stood transfixed by strain.
I sang some words I did not know...
And have forgot again.

I know he sang... but how
That fragile web of skin and bone
Could pour forth life...
I do not know...

I only know
I heard a swan song...
Confirming legends
Of a thousand years.

Tony,
The second man, his son
Who hunted with him...
Died that fall
In a car accident...

The night before he died, we talked
And drank and smoked...
He told us how he was prepared for hunting...
His boots, his coat, his gun...
He dreamed of meat for the winter.
His pride was in his skill.

He was lean and dark as a shadow...
A Spirit of the wood.
No school could hold him
But he could read the trail.

He lit three cigarettes before he left...
A round of three... a sniper's danger sign.
I almost blew the third one out...
as though I knew.
"I'm going back o'town," he said.
In two hours he was dead.

Buncie,
His friend,
Died the next weekend, near the same hour...
In the same way...
When Tony died, he had cried
"Tony has kids and wife
I've had a life.
Why wasn't it me?"

And so it was.

He lived through Korea, the fifties war,
And nine years of prison...
No, I don't know what for.
Then three years back
He lived glad... day to day...
He died no less courageous,
But more knowing.
Some men learn from having, he, from lack,
Knew all there was to life...

I can see him yet,
Sunlit, upon the road...

"Mag, lend me a dollar for wine."
His cigarettes in his boot,
His wave, and his smile.
Each day was his last,
Each walk, his last mile.

I saw three friends die
From June to November...
In a few years,
Will no one remember?

LITTLE WOLF WAS HUNTING DOGS

Little Wolf was hunting dogs.
        The wild dogs
        The April dogs
That go mad in summer.

He was shooting dogs
        Along the quiet road
        In Ponemah

By mistake,
He shot a child.
A small child
Who was hiding like a fox.
Who was hiding from
The fourth grade
In the brush
In the warm April sun
        In Ponemah.

The child is safe now
Safe from spelling and corrections
Safe from fractions forever
Safe from girls and growing up
Safe from school
        In Ponemah

SAM WELEFSKY

Sam, the tailor
Cutter by trade,
Cutter of canvas
For the armies of the Republic.
Tent cutter
Parachute cutter
Pants cutter
Patterns of pants.
Trousers, slacks.
Sam
With his round eye-glasses
And his round stoop.
Back to the sun...

His life laid out in patterns
On the cutting table.

Thirty years from his immigration
Sam bought the corporation...
President Sam.

He lives with his mother
And his huge samovar
In his automatic palace
Where the rich folks are.

His mother
Plants tomatoes
With the flowers
For their own sake...
"Because they are beautiful and round."

The ghosts of old Russian famines
Make no sound
As they move through the cannas
And tomatoes
Near his house
By the lake.

A MURRAY COUNTY FARM

The Santee walked this land
Two hundred years ago.
Now they are gone.

The road winds down
Past Buffalo Ridge.
The land is taut,
A well stretched drum,
But only the sun
Beats down on the corn:

Yellow field
Green field
Yellow field
Brown
Yellow Field
Green Field
Yellow Field
Brown.

Down from the top of Buffalo Ridge
Down to the lake
Where the Fur Trade Post
Has shrunk
To a nail and a sign.

And the pipestone mine
Is a national monument.

One hundred years ago
This land became a farm.

The walnut grove,
Straight planted
Tall.
Empty of all
But walnut trees.

The house is white.
The barn is red.
The farmer greeted me
And said,
"*Come in. Come in!*"
He moves the chair
For me.
His mind is quick
As a dog in the corn.
His face is burned
And his hands are worn.
He talks of taxes
"*Divided fair.*"
He smiles with pride.
"*For the people make the laws
In Murray County.*"

Alma, his wife
Is tall and reserved.
A secret field
In summer.

We walk to the barn
With rafters forty feet above the floor.
A castle.
Storage for the hay.
Cattle food and children's play.
Safe and warm
On a rainy day.

Two cows she milks.
"*Enough for us.*"
Two grown boys
She has, but they are gone.
"*The cows know me,*"
She laughs and says, "*They know.*"
They stand as patiently
As she.

Beneath her hand
The farm has moved
From its beginning.
With quiet and with graceful tread
She moves to see the chickens fed
And watered and let out to run...

Alma and Henry
Last of this world too.
Together with
The trapper
And the Santee Sioux.

This land half hung with silence,
Half with dreams.
The old dog, hopeful, and the sun.
The morning sun upon the sheep
In that south pasture... pointed herd
Grazing East.
        The magnet earth
        Holds orbit for the astronaut
        Another bridge of time.

New covered wagons come.

4

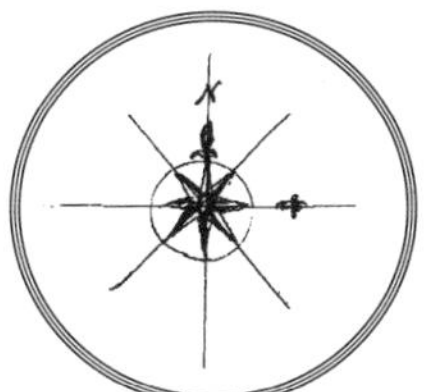

YOU CANNOT CAGE A BUTTERFLY

You cannot cage a butterfly.
It beats its wings and soon will die.

But when it rides the silver air,
All heaven shouts...
        See there...
                See there!

But you may build a firefly's cage
For in its body beauties rage.

Untouched by bars, its wings.
For they are smaller things...

One lights the earth.
        The other, the sky.

                Which can I?

COMMUNITY

We can speak of hungers of the soul.
We are not friends or lovers,
But segments of a larger whole,
Bonded by integrity.

Yes.
You can speak to me
Of God, or Trinity,

Or just about that tree
That shakes in ecstasy...
Because its winds are free.

And I can nod my head
Without surprise
And say,
"I see."

TEXTURES

Cool Stones
And shells
And beads
And bells
Clouds
Pearl button grey
Smoothly
Closing up the day.
And sheets of blue and snow
Taut stretched
Across a bed I know.
And marble
Tombstones too
Are of this spirit -
Calm and new
But still eternal
Textures.

Like an endless line
Linking all the
Senses that are mine.

THE END OF LEARNING

On the desert of the mind
I quarry out the stone
But the structure is unknown...
Though I strive to find
The burnished shine
Of metal
But there is no sign.

I followed all the
Unstarred maps...

I do not understand.
The universe
Is larger than I planned
Perhaps..

Take back the books and compass.
I search no more
For day is done.

Call down the dove
And send for that small olive branch
From faith's far shore.
I need its green and reassuring glance...

The shaded quarry pit
May fill once more

With God's true light...
The shadows wake
Now I may turn
          and see...
I stand
Unchained.

How wide
Is the arc
Of Eternity!

EUCHARIST

...He placed at the east of the Garden of Eden, Cherubim, and a flaming sword which turned every way to keep the way of the tree of life.

Genesis 3:24

...lest he put forth his hand and take and eat of the tree of life and live forever.

Genesis 3:22

I wonder, in the Garden, about that other tree,
The one from which they ate no fruit
Or didn't even see...

It was so long ago
We have forgot
What is Good and Evil too.

"Forgive them for they
Know not what they do."

Perhaps it was the Cross that stood
        Hidden in that ancient wood.

No leafy green
        No flaming sword
Now comes between
        No guarding Cherubim
Is seen.

They could have eaten from it
        He forbade them only one.

Now our fruit is bread and wine:
        Jesus Christ, His Son.

THIS VERY FLESH

Ecclesiastes:
And desire shall fail, because man goeth to his long home and the mourners go about the streets...
Or ever the silver cord be loosed or the golden bowl be broken, or the pitcher be broken at the fountain,or the wheel be broken at the cistern... Then shall the dust return to the earth as it was, and the spirit shall return to God who gave it.

This very flesh
        That rings me round
And mingles with my mind
Will drop as leaves in Autumn...
        I also find
        "All flesh is grass"
The prophets truly cry...

I turn toward the summer sky
Or walk along the beach, or swim.
I finger stones
And hold a child
I talk with friends
And watch the sun...
        "All flesh is one"

This pulsing moving I
And firm sweet apples
And the buzzing fly

Will sink together under sands
While our small world will drop...
A bead upon a stranded universe.

Of course I love the morning and the night
And all time in between
This banquet of existence
And the hermit's cell...

You hope for heaven?
I wish you well.

DO I GROW STRONGER STILL

Do I grow stronger still
        But to sustain a larger wound?
Does my small sense of springtime
        Wake for only winter's cold?

And, fingering the hangman's hank of
        Old old rope
Against my spent youth,
        I wonder at
My solemn search for truth.

        A wandering down
Some littered alley of lean lies...
My childhood lost in simple gazing
        At the skies
Now beclouded by the factory smoke...

You say, "It's all a joke,
        Not rightly taken?"

I hope you are again mistaken.

I like the sound...
"*A live hound is better than a dead lion.*"

The bees that swarm and feed
Do not brew so strong a mead
        To wake him... Yes.
The Baalish temple fell
The deed is best... though blind
The jackal's cry is better than the silence...

I
shall not stop
From staring at the sky...
Nor fingering the apple blossoms
Under the sun's strong eye...
Nor laughing at some symbol
        Struck from Socrates
And seeded in the heart's warm earth...

I shall seek this splendor...
Though the hair shirt shall be worn...
And *the day of my death be better*
Than the day that I was born.

ANUBIS

The cry of hounds sounds Death...
        The ancient cries...
Anubis and the hood
        The fear of full pursuit
        Through moonlit wood
Rings down this day.

        To peopled cities
        And the stray that howls..
        Starts fear.

        The siren sounds
        That speed
        Wake those who lie

In full possession of their blood
        All warm...
        But
        What is safety in their bed?

        What covers hide from Him?

A PRAYER

Give me a dream
That I may keep
Forever as my goal.
And always before me
Make it to leap
Urging onward my soul.

For dreams I know
Are tender things
That break at any touch...
Give me a dream
With faster wings
Although
I want it much.

WATER POURED

Water poured
Upon a stone
Runs off and leaves
The stone the same
Thus it should be
With fame.

Water poured
Upon a clod
Sinks in, around
Below, above,
Brings bright new life
Into the sod,
And thus it is
With love.

FLOWERS FRESH GATHERED

Does Death now walk exulting
        Through the fields
Bearing you tenderly
As I have carried flowers...
In remembrance of past hours?

Does Death now hold you close
        Crushing the fragrance
Of your soft passing...
        Distillations of all dead...
Does Death cry low
Upon his bed
For loves lost days...
And later through the haze of time
Does Death cast you out
Faded husk and bloom
Past comets and constellations...
        Where is your final room?

IT IS LATE

It is late
But I have seen a vision.
Truth slipped in between
The pillars of the room
The paragraph portrayed
A flame... a moment's light
Upon the wall.
It's gone again!

REVELATION

I take my wine
In little sips
For I have seen
Apocalypse.

About the Author

Maggie Smith was born in 1927 in Medicine Hat, Alberta, Canada. Her early years were spent on her father's sheep ranch near Bow Island. Her family later moved to Arkansas and then returned to Choteau, Montana where her parents had spent their early years. Upon the death of her parents when she was sixteen, she lived with relatives in northern Alberta but returned to Choteau to complete her high school education.

Upon her marriage to D. David Smith, Maggie moved to Minneapolis, Minnesota where her daughter, Margaret, was born. Although she has traveled widely, Minneapolis has remained her home. Throughout her life, an important source of spiritual strength has been her association with the Episcopal Church community in Minneapolis.

Over the years, Maggie has held a variety of jobs , from office work to serving as a Laboratory Administrator for Medtronic Corp. For several years, she was the Director of Community Education at the Red Lake Indian Reservation. In 1995 she retired from Medtronic after a number of years as a Security Supervisor. In the same year, she also graduated magna cum laude from the University of Minnesota with a degree in anthropology. She is now working on several anthropological projects.